IF FOUND, PLEASE RETURN TO

NAME

CONTACT

THE PROPERTY INVESTOR'S DAILY PLANNER

ABOUT THE PLANNER...

When you're in the business of property, it's easy to become busy, overworked and feeling like you're not making progress.

What is sold as a 'passive income' dream can soon suck up more time than you ever thought and you can find yourself elbow-deep in regulation, property maintenance issues and nearing burn out. Instead of living the dream you end up in a property nightmare.

This daily planner provides you the prompts, reminders and motivation you need to to take action on your chosen property strategy and achieve your goals.

The front section encourages you to be crystal clear on why you are in property, how it contributes to your life goals, the skills you need to be successful and where to get help.

The daily planner motivates you to focus on key tasks and meetings by reminding you of WHY you are doing this. It also encourages you to recognise your achievements along the way and think of the other people benefiting from your ongoing success.

With a clear set of objectives and an organised approach you will soon have smashed your property goals.

When the WHY is clear,
the HOW is easy

WHAT'S YOUR *WHY?*

My life's purpose and my personal goals are...

The property goals that will help me achieve my life goals are...

WHAT'S YOUR HOW?

My main property strategy is...

The daily, weekly and monthly actions I will take to achieve this are...

WHO'S ON YOUR TEAM?

My Accountant / Bookkeeper is... and the services they provide are...

My Solicitor is... and the services they provide are...

My Mortgage Broker is... and the services they provide are...

WHO'S ON YOUR TEAM?

My Estate Agents / Letting Agents are... and the services they provide are...

My Builder / Tradesmen / Project Manager

Other specialists, e.g. Architect, Planning Consultant,

SKILLS & KNOWLEDGE

The property knowledge and skills gaps I have are...

The way I will fill these gaps is by...

NETWORKING

The value I have to offer other property investors is...

The benefits I would like to gain from networking are...

The networking events I will attend are...

PROPERTY FOCUS

The 4 properties at the top of my shortlist, and my next action...

PROPERTY FOCUS

The 4 properties at the top of my shortlist, and my next action...

PROPERTY FOCUS

The 4 properties at the top of my shortlist, and my next action...

PROPERTY FOCUS

The 4 properties at the top of my shortlist, and my next action...

NOTES

TODAY'S AGENDA
DATE:

To-Do List   **Key Meetings**

My motivation for today: An Inspirational Quotation...

NOTES

TODAY'S AGENDA

DATE:

To-Do List

Key Meetings

My motivation for today: What's my WHY?

NOTES

TODAY'S AGENDA

DATE:

To-Do List   **Key Meetings**

My motivation for today: Which of my end-goals am I working on today?

NOTES

TODAY'S AGENDA
DATE:

To-Do List   **Key Meetings**

My motivation for today: Who needs me on my A-Game?

NOTES

TODAY'S AGENDA

DATE:

To-Do List   **Key Meetings**

My motivation for today: What results am I starting to see?

NOTES

TODAY'S AGENDA

DATE:

To-Do List   Key Meetings

My motivation for today: What challenge did I overcome in the last week?

NOTES

TODAY'S AGENDA
DATE:

To-Do List   **Key Meetings**

My motivation for today: How am I helping others this week?

NOTES

TODAY'S AGENDA
DATE:

To-Do List   **Key Meetings**

My motivation for today: An Inspirational Quotation...

NOTES

TODAY'S AGENDA

DATE:

To-Do List   **Key Meetings**

My motivation for today: What's my WHY?

NOTES

TODAY'S AGENDA
DATE:

To-Do List   **Key Meetings**

My motivation for today: Which of my end-goals am I working on today?

NOTES

TODAY'S AGENDA
DATE:

To-Do List   **Key Meetings**

My motivation for today: Who needs me on my A-Game?

NOTES

TODAY'S AGENDA
DATE:

To-Do List   **Key Meetings**

My motivation for today: What results am I starting to see?

NOTES

TODAY'S AGENDA

DATE:

To-Do List   Key Meetings

My motivation for today: What challenge did I overcome in the last week?

NOTES

TODAY'S AGENDA
DATE:

To-Do List   **Key Meetings**

My motivation for today: How am I helping others this week?

NOTES

TODAY'S AGENDA
DATE:

To-Do List   **Key Meetings**

My motivation for today: An Inspirational Quotation...

NOTES

TODAY'S AGENDA
DATE:

To-Do List   **Key Meetings**

My motivation for today: What's my WHY?

NOTES

TODAY'S AGENDA

DATE:

To-Do List   Key Meetings

My motivation for today: Which of my end-goals am I working on today?

NOTES

TODAY'S AGENDA
DATE:

To-Do List   **Key Meetings**

My motivation for today: Who needs me on my A-Game?

NOTES

TODAY'S AGENDA
DATE:

To-Do List   **Key Meetings**

My motivation for today: What results am I starting to see?

NOTES

TODAY'S AGENDA

DATE:

To-Do List   Key Meetings

My motivation for today: What challenge did I overcome in the last week?

NOTES

TODAY'S AGENDA
DATE:

To-Do List   **Key Meetings**

My motivation for today: How am I helping others this week?

NOTES

TODAY'S AGENDA
DATE:

To-Do List   **Key Meetings**

My motivation for today: An Inspirational Quotation...

NOTES

TODAY'S AGENDA

DATE:

To-Do List   **Key Meetings**

My motivation for today: What's my WHY?

NOTES

TODAY'S AGENDA
DATE:

To-Do List   **Key Meetings**

My motivation for today: Which of my end-goals am I working on today?

NOTES

TODAY'S AGENDA

DATE:

To-Do List

Key Meetings

My motivation for today: Who needs me on my A-Game?

NOTES

TODAY'S AGENDA
DATE:

To-Do List   **Key Meetings**

My motivation for today: What results am I starting to see?

NOTES

TODAY'S AGENDA
DATE:

To-Do List   **Key Meetings**

My motivation for today: What challenge did I overcome in the last week?

NOTES

TODAY'S AGENDA
DATE:

To-Do List   Key Meetings

My motivation for today: How am I helping others this week?

NOTES

TODAY'S AGENDA
DATE:

To-Do List

Key Meetings

My motivation for today: An Inspirational Quotation...

NOTES

TODAY'S AGENDA
DATE:

To-Do List   **Key Meetings**

My motivation for today: What's my WHY?

NOTES

TODAY'S AGENDA

DATE:

To-Do List   Key Meetings

My motivation for today: Which of my end-goals am I working on today?

NOTES

TODAY'S AGENDA

DATE:

To-Do List   **Key Meetings**

My motivation for today: Who needs me on my A-Game?

NOTES

TODAY'S AGENDA
DATE:

To-Do List   **Key Meetings**

My motivation for today: What results am I starting to see?

NOTES

TODAY'S AGENDA

DATE:

To-Do List   Key Meetings

My motivation for today: What challenge did I overcome in the last week?

NOTES

TODAY'S AGENDA
DATE:

To-Do List   **Key Meetings**

My motivation for today: How am I helping others this week?

NOTES

TODAY'S AGENDA
DATE:

To-Do List   **Key Meetings**

My motivation for today: An Inspirational Quotation...

NOTES

TODAY'S AGENDA
DATE:

To-Do List   Key Meetings

My motivation for today: What's my bigger WHY?

NOTES

TODAY'S AGENDA
DATE:

To-Do List   Key Meetings

My motivation for today: Which of my end-goals am I working on today?

NOTES

TODAY'S AGENDA
DATE:

To-Do List

Key Meetings

My motivation for today: Who needs me on my A-Game?

NOTES

TODAY'S AGENDA

DATE:

To-Do List   **Key Meetings**

My motivation for today: What results am I starting to see?

NOTES

TODAY'S AGENDA

DATE:

To-Do List   Key Meetings

My motivation for today: What challenge did I overcome in the last week?

NOTES

TODAY'S AGENDA
DATE:

To-Do List   **Key Meetings**

My motivation for today: How am I helping others this week?

NOTES

TODAY'S AGENDA

DATE:

To-Do List   **Key Meetings**

My motivation for today: An Inspirational Quotation...

NOTES

TODAY'S AGENDA
DATE:

To-Do List **Key Meetings**

My motivation for today: What's my WHY?

NOTES

TODAY'S AGENDA
DATE:

To-Do List   **Key Meetings**

My motivation for today: Which of my end-goals am I working on today?

NOTES

TODAY'S AGENDA
DATE:

To-Do List   **Key Meetings**

My motivation for today: Who needs me on my A-Game?

NOTES

TODAY'S AGENDA

DATE:

To-Do List   **Key Meetings**

My motivation for today: What results am I starting to see?

NOTES

TODAY'S AGENDA
DATE:

To-Do List   Key Meetings

My motivation for today: What challenge did I overcome in the last week?

NOTES

TODAY'S AGENDA

DATE:

To-Do List   Key Meetings

My motivation for today: How am I helping others this week?

NOTES

TODAY'S AGENDA
DATE:

To-Do List   **Key Meetings**

My motivation for today: An Inspirational Quotation...

NOTES

TODAY'S AGENDA

DATE:

To-Do List   **Key Meetings**

My motivation for today: What's my WHY?

NOTES

TODAY'S AGENDA

DATE:

To-Do List

Key Meetings

My motivation for today: Which of my end-goals am I working on today?

NOTES

TODAY'S AGENDA

DATE:

To-Do List   **Key Meetings**

My motivation for today: Who needs me on my A-Game?

NOTES

TODAY'S AGENDA
DATE:

To-Do List   **Key Meetings**

My motivation for today: What results am I starting to see?

NOTES

TODAY'S AGENDA
DATE:

To-Do List   **Key Meetings**

My motivation for today: What challenge did I overcome in the last week?

NOTES

TODAY'S AGENDA
DATE:

To-Do List   **Key Meetings**

My motivation for today: How am I helping others this week?

NOTES

TODAY'S AGENDA
DATE:

To-Do List   **Key Meetings**

My motivation for today: An Inspirational Quotation...

NOTES

TODAY'S AGENDA

DATE:

To-Do List   **Key Meetings**

My motivation for today: What's my WHY?

NOTES

TODAY'S AGENDA

DATE:

To-Do List   Key Meetings

My motivation for today: Which of my end-goals am I working on today?

NOTES

TODAY'S AGENDA
DATE:

To-Do List   **Key Meetings**

My motivation for today: Who needs me on my A-Game?

NOTES

TODAY'S AGENDA

DATE:

To-Do List   **Key Meetings**

My motivation for today: What results am I starting to see?

NOTES

TODAY'S AGENDA
DATE:

To-Do List   Key Meetings

My motivation for today: What challenge did I overcome in the last week?

NOTES

TODAY'S AGENDA

DATE:

To-Do List   **Key Meetings**

My motivation for today: How am I helping others this week?

NOTES

TODAY'S AGENDA
DATE:

To-Do List   **Key Meetings**

My motivation for today: An Inspirational Quotation...

NOTES

TODAY'S AGENDA

DATE:

To-Do List   **Key Meetings**

My motivation for today: What's my WHY?

NOTES

TODAY'S AGENDA

DATE:

To-Do List   Key Meetings

My motivation for today: Which of my end-goals am I working on today?

NOTES

TODAY'S AGENDA

DATE:

To-Do List   Key Meetings

My motivation for today: Who needs me on my A-Game?

NOTES

TODAY'S AGENDA

DATE:

To-Do List   **Key Meetings**

My motivation for today: What results am I starting to see?

NOTES

TODAY'S AGENDA
DATE:

To-Do List   Key Meetings

My motivation for today: What challenge did I overcome in the last week?

NOTES

TODAY'S AGENDA
DATE:

To-Do List   Key Meetings

My motivation for today: How am I helping others this week?

NOTES

TODAY'S AGENDA
DATE:

To-Do List   **Key Meetings**

My motivation for today: An Inspirational Quotation...

NOTES

TODAY'S AGENDA

DATE:

To-Do List   **Key Meetings**

My motivation for today: What's my WHY?

NOTES

TODAY'S AGENDA

DATE:

To-Do List   Key Meetings

My motivation for today: Which of my end-goals am I working on today?

NOTES

TODAY'S AGENDA

DATE:

To-Do List   **Key Meetings**

My motivation for today: Who needs me on my A-Game?

NOTES

TODAY'S AGENDA

DATE:

To-Do List   Key Meetings

My motivation for today: What results am I starting to see?

NOTES

TODAY'S AGENDA
DATE:

To-Do List   Key Meetings

My motivation for today: What challenge did I overcome in the last week?

NOTES

TODAY'S AGENDA
DATE:

To-Do List   **Key Meetings**

My motivation for today: How am I helping others this week?

NOTES

TODAY'S AGENDA
DATE:

To-Do List   **Key Meetings**

My motivation for today: An Inspirational Quotation...

NOTES

TODAY'S AGENDA

DATE:

To-Do List   Key Meetings

My motivation for today: What's my WHY?

NOTES

TODAY'S AGENDA

DATE:

To-Do List   **Key Meetings**

My motivation for today: Which of my end-goals am I working on today?

NOTES

TODAY'S AGENDA

DATE:

To-Do List   **Key Meetings**

My motivation for today: Who needs me on my A-Game?

NOTES

TODAY'S AGENDA

DATE:

To-Do List   Key Meetings

My motivation for today: What results am I starting to see?

NOTES

TODAY'S AGENDA
DATE:

To-Do List   Key Meetings

My motivation for today: What challenge did I overcome in the last week?

NOTES

TODAY'S AGENDA
DATE:

To-Do List   **Key Meetings**

My motivation for today: How am I helping others this week?

NOTES

TODAY'S AGENDA

DATE:

To-Do List   Key Meetings

My motivation for today: An Inspirational Quotation...

NOTES

TODAY'S AGENDA

DATE:

To-Do List   **Key Meetings**

My motivation for today: What's my WHY?

NOTES

TODAY'S AGENDA

DATE:

To-Do List

Key Meetings

My motivation for today: Which of my end-goals am I working on today?

NOTES

TODAY'S AGENDA
DATE:

To-Do List   Key Meetings

My motivation for today: Who needs me on my A-Game?

NOTES

TODAY'S AGENDA

DATE:

To-Do List   Key Meetings

My motivation for today: What results am I starting to see?

NOTES

TODAY'S AGENDA
DATE:

To-Do List   **Key Meetings**

My motivation for today: What challenge did I overcome in the last week?

NOTES

TODAY'S AGENDA
DATE:

To-Do List   Key Meetings

My motivation for today: How am I helping others this week?

NOTES

UK PROPERTY RESOURCES

BOOKS
The Complete Guide to Property Investing, Rob Dix
Property Magic, Simon Zutshi
Property Investment Hacking, John Wilson
Rent to Rent, Jacqui Edwards
Commercial Property Conversions, Mark Homer & Glenn Delve

PODCASTS
The Property Podcast
Property Magic
Mark my Words
Inside property investing

NETWORKING
Progressive Property Network (PPN) - Nationwide
Property Investors Network (PIN) - Nationwide
Baker Street Property Meet - London
Saj Hussains Property Meet - Birmingham

APPS & WEBSITES
Rightmove.co.uk
Openrent.co.uk
Spareroom.co.uk
Nethouseprices.com
Mouseprice.com
Floorplanner.com
Gotenant.co.uk
Propertylink.estatesgazette.com
Progressiveproperty.co.uk
Propertyinvestorsnetwork.co.uk
Cashflow-freedom.co.uk

NOTES